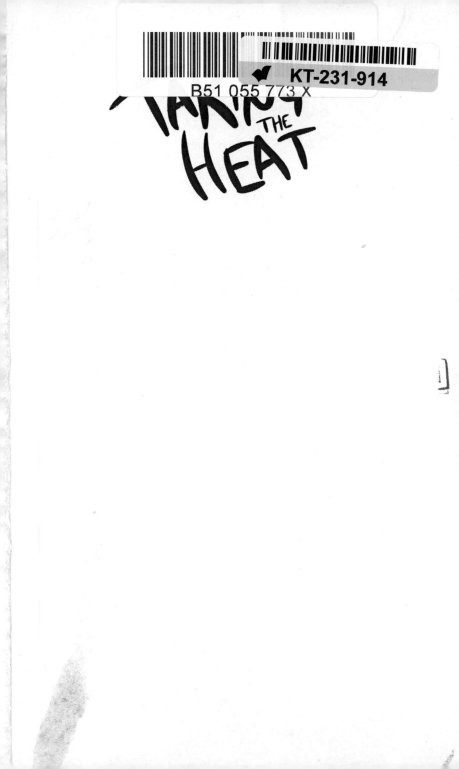

KT-231-914

TAKING
THE
HEAT

TAKING THE HEAT

NICK SNELLING

NativeSpain.™com

First Published in Great Britain 2008 by www.BookShaker.com

© Copyright Nick Snelling

Typeset in Book Antiqua

Illustrated by Margaret Denmark

To my nomadic family - may our movements be always both regular and successful.

Praise For This Book

"A side-splitting account of life in Spain."
The Xpat Magazine
www.thexpat.com

"Casa Desolada is rather a jolly place despite the author's attempts to convince us otherwise in this Brysonesque take on the lot of the beleaguered expat."
Theresa O'Shea
Co-author of 'In the Garlic: Your Informative,
fun Guide to Spain', www.inthegarlic.com

"An hilarious introduction to life in Spain and the disastrous goings-on in Casa Desolada. Recounted by Nick Snelling and wittily illustrated by Margaret Denmark this book is "Just William" in long trousers! Do read it."
Herbert Wise
Director of 'I Claudius', 'Rumpole of The Bailey',
'Inspector Morse', 'A Touch of Frost' and others...

Foreword

The challenges of starting a new life in a foreign country will be familiar to many people reading this book. If they are not - don't worry, you're in for a treat someday. A new home, a new language, a new school for the kids, a new job... the list goes on. There are inevitably a few bumps and bruises on the way, but retaining a sense of humour - as Nick will tell you - is the key. And this book will most definitely help you do that.

Genuine laugh-out-loud prose is a rarity these days, but this little nugget of a book is full of it. Whether it's a doomed family trip to the beach or a shopping excursion from hell, Nick always manages to capture the despair quite perfectly. Most readers will see themselves in here somewhere; and by laughing at Nick, we are by proxy laughing at ourselves. Which is never a bad thing...

Gary Cohen, October 2008

Contents

A Flood of Advice

Before leaving the UK to live in Spain, I was offered all types of advice. Apart from not drinking the water, I was told that I would never get anything done, that I would have terrible trouble coming to terms with having no seasons and that I would live in fear of my new home being land-grabbed at the very earliest opportunity.

Worse still, I was warned that my new life would fall apart unless I had an unquenchable penchant for sangria and bullfighting. Frankly, this was a load of old rot.

When you leave the UK you only need one piece of advice, irrespective of the country, whether it is a Caribbean island, Iraq or Spain itself. It is advice so critical that the success of any relocation is intimately bound up in following it exactly: "Only ever buy a house within easy walking distance of a friendly, English speaking plumber." It is that simple. Nothing else matters.

Like most men, I am an ardent DIY fiddler with a vastly over-optimistic regard for his paltry skills. Invariably, I feel that my very manhood is at stake when my wife mentions, for example, that she has noticed a tiny leak on a pipe. Dismissing her sound advice to call in a plumber, I will tackle a leaking pipe with the lunatic confidence of someone truly out of their depth whose machismo has been darkly questioned.

My DIY plumbing is almost always begun early on a Sunday morning, whilst everyone else is still in bed and well before my wife can spot what I am doing. Inevitably, my efforts are followed by some seemingly unrelated connector completely parting company with the rest of the pipework to produce a leak of simply epic proportions.

Margaret Denmark

The result is predictable as my family are roused by my screams of appalled terror and arrive to see an unsuccessful recreation of the Dutch boy trying to stem the flood coming in through the dyke. In fact, of course, that is as far as the resemblance goes. For starters, the Dutch boy lacked a wife whose enraged gaze alone could halt a runaway juggernaut and, unlike me, he was not left trying to stem the flow of a central heating pipe full of super-high pressure, scalding water.

In fact, I reckon the Dutch boy had things all his own way. He did not have to battle in a foreign language, fast vanishing under the stress of the occasion, for a recalcitrant Valencian plumber. Neither was he distracted by the dire financial implications of his actions.

In the UK it is almost impossible to find a plumber in an emergency and, when you do, you know that you are in for a financial commitment that would make an investment banker blanch. Over here, things can be just as bad, with any negotiating leverage being minimal when you are up to your knees in water and over your head when it comes to dealing with an incandescent wife.

All of a sudden, your dream retirement can spiral into a vortex of disaster, simply because you moved nowhere near a friendly plumber. You will find that your marital rights were, in fact, merely discretionary and your dream villa will be quickly replaced by a small room in the local home for the displaced.

It just is not worth taking the risk.

When I bought Casa Desolada, the Gods must have been smiling down upon me. To my unspeakable delight a new neighbour, Harry, turned out to be a retired plumber. And not just a plumber but also a friendly English one, with a tolerance and kindness that has sustained me through several traumatic crises. As a direct consequence, my marriage remains largely intact and my tenuous occupation of the marital home reasonably secure. Give or take.

I say 'give or take' as Harry has mentioned moving recently. We are delightfully happy where we are, but there is no question that we will follow him. Indeed, I am already planning the move, although I have yet to tell my wife that Harry wants to go to Chechnya. This may be something of a problem but I know good advice when I hear it and, from now on, where Harry goes, I go too.

A Signal Failure

I wonder if I am the only Briton not to have satellite TV in Spain? I suspect so, as everyone except me appears to be thoroughly well informed and anyone I meet treats me as a complete dimwit.

In my more sanguine moments, I can see where they are coming from. I have not the remotest idea about current world events and my knowledge of soap opera theatrics is totally non-existent. Indeed, the only in-coming information that I receive from the wider world is restricted to ageing copies of the Daily Mail that I occasionally fall across from our redundant removal packaging. Having a conversation with me is, I am unkindly advised, rather like encountering a time warp.

You may ask why I lack satellite TV, despite the urgent entreaties of my lady wife, the begging cries of despair from my children and my own gathering recognition that I now know nothing about anything?

Well, I have made a stand. A stand on a matter of deep principle, as the head of my own household.

This is no small matter, as I have been searching fruitlessly for twenty years for a matter of principle upon which I could assert my patriarchal authority. I have been constantly ignored in the past by my family, who have treated my 'points of principle' as utterly irrelevant eccentricities. Indeed, my position within the family food chain has descended remorselessly to just above that of the cat which, being a stray, indicates more than I like to admit in public about my status.

Margaret Denmark

However, I am nothing if not a fighter and I have chosen the crusade of not having satellite TV as the necessary route to reasserting my authority. After all, am I not the senior male of the household? Is it not me who is, occasionally, the breadwinner?

More to the point, is it not me who has to go up on the roof to fix the satellite dish? A small task, you may say, however you have not seen Casa Desolada any more, thinking about it, than did a surveyor before we bought it. It has the structural integrity of a rusting caravan and could no more bear the weight of a satellite dish than the proverbial donkey another stalk of straw.

I have told my wife nothing of this, of course, primarily because the choice of house was largely mine. She still believes my assertions that the house is built so well that it could take the full force of a nuclear explosion rather than the truth, which is that it probably already has.

Anyone who thinks I am going to step onto the top of my roof is gravely mistaken. I still value my life and the last thing I want is to find that the first satellite news programme to be seen by my family will be dedicated to the lunacy of their late husband and father. Anyway, in the unlikely event the house was able to support a satellite dish, I fear that it would effectively act like a sail and wrench the house from its pitiful foundations. We have enough trouble with the post as it is, without the position of the front door changing on a minute-by-minute basis.

No, for the time being, satellite TV is bad. Very bad indeed. There are simply too many programmes available. As to the news and documentaries? Well, they are superfluous and all the information required for a fulfilling life can surely be gained from reading the classics and a few yellowing newspapers.

Mind you, to prove that I am a broadminded and flexible family member, I have been working hard recently with a friend of mine who has the full range of satellite TV. Both he and I believe that if we watch long enough, a film about the renovation of properties that were near the ground zero of an atomic bomb will appear. So far, we have had little success and I have had to endure hours of sports programmes, documentaries and films.

Obviously, it is hard work watching satellite TV, but someone in the family must force themselves to do it. And, in the truest spirit of self-sacrifice, I am proud to say that I have risen to the occasion, notwithstanding the curious fury of my wife and children.

Burnt Out

I cannot, for the life of me, fathom why barbecues are so popular. Indeed, I can honestly say that some of the worst food I have ever tasted has been at barbecues, most of it, unfortunately, cooked by myself.

Even when I have not been directly involved in the cooking, I have often been handed meat that a decent vet could probably have resuscitated with the right equipment. Only sheer hunger and blurred vision from clouds of swirling smoke have prevented me from realising this until far, far too late. By the time the charcoal goes out, I am invariably looking anxiously towards the nearest bathroom in anticipation of the first dramatic symptoms of chronic food poisoning.

Barbecues are an inevitable disaster as, for some primeval reason, it is always a man that does the cooking. Invariably, he is the least well qualified person to cook anything, let alone for a party of twenty starving guests. This would be a major undertaking for most women but for the average man, who never sees the inside of a kitchen from one day to the next, it is akin to a bicycle repairer constructing the engines of Challenger 2.

At Casa Desolada, barbecues, to the common relief of our few remaining friends, have been banned. This may seem a little dramatic but I simply cannot look the A and E doctors of our local hospital in the eye any longer. They know exactly the problem when my family and friends arrive, at roughly the same time, suffering identical symptoms, whilst looking savagely and very obviously at me.

There has, of course, been a terrible misunderstanding.

Margaret Devinagh

Men, in ancient times, never did the cooking. We were the hunter gatherers and would take our day's haul back to our grateful women to cook, whilst we rested from our labours. The incontrovertible evidence for this can be seen in any child's picture book. Exhausted from fighting off dinosaurs, cave men can always be seen watching their womenfolk happily spitting food over an open fire. This is, surely, the natural and proper way.

As I have stated many times to my wife, I am a hunter gatherer not a caterer and barbecues, with me as the cook, offend my deepest instincts. Sadly, my wife's respect for my abilities as a hunter, are not what they should be. Indeed, she is apt to remind me, stingingly, that the last time I hunted anything it had a skirt on, took two years to capture, put up a bruising fight and has remained alive and in charge for the past twenty.

My wife is equally dismissive of my gathering capabilities despite my annual blackberry and mushroom expeditions which, admittedly, tend to yield a rather erratic crop. Invariably, it is the wrong season when I boldly set off into the unforgiving wilderness, only to find that the shops are poorly stocked and the surrounding bars too enticing. Stinking of alcohol and carrying a couple of apples, my last return prompted my wife to refute generations of intensive research undertaken by the world's most eminent anthropologists. She now mistakenly seems to believe that women have always done all the work and that men are completely useless.

She is being a little unfair, of course. Only last month I put up a shelf and nearly helped her carry the week's rubbish down to the bins. Previous to that, I had given her invaluable advice about where to put the oil in the car and the ideal pressure for the tyres. This is help that I would have welcomed with an open heart, had I been in her situation.

Clearly, us men must unite. Burn the barbecues, I say, and let us return to the natural order! Our credibility is at stake and we must act before the irons go in the fire again and whilst we still have the stomach for the job. We did not come to Spain to test their national health service and have sausages spit at us! No, we must rid ourselves of these enslaving implements and regain our position as masters of our own households.

Road To Romance

When it comes to travel, I am nothing if not a romantic. I hate the concept of pre-planning trips and organising beforehand a schedule of places to stay. For me, the joy of travelling is immeasurably enhanced by the spontaneity of exploration and the unexpected wonder created by finding somewhere previously unknown. This is, surely, the true spirit of romance. It runs deep in my veins.

To my wife, unfortunately, it seems that it is not so much the spirit of romance that runs through my veins, as a dangerously high octane mixture of far too much alcohol and the undiluted genes of someone terminally irresponsible. This is a touch unfair.

After all, we do not always end up struggling desperately to erect a tent at midnight on council waste ground during a rainstorm. I can think of at least one occasion when we found somewhere pleasant to stay before darkness fell. From memory, it occurred some years ago on a summer holiday close to the Arctic Circle in Norway. But the female psyche is nothing if not unforgiving and, over the years, this reassuring success has been conveniently forgotten.

Perhaps, due to this slip of memory, my impulsive decisions to take off on the spur of the moment are invariably sabotaged by my wife's packing of our car. Certainly, I have never seen a vehicle readied so assiduously, at the least hint of a trip out. With a suspicion lacking any trace of optimism, my wife invariably packs sufficient supplies and clothing to sustain the family through the long term after-affects of a nuclear war.

Inevitably, we start off at least three hours later than envisaged, with our car struggling under a load more normally associated with a concrete lorry. Even downhill, our speed rarely reaches that required to overtake a peasant farmer on a three wheeled tractor. This is not helpful, when my dream is to motor gaily down the open road with the intention of unexpectedly finding somewhere remote and romantic, with sufficient time to watch the sun drop lazily below the horizon.

The last time we lumbered down the high speed roads of Spain we were headed for Albarracín, a delightful medieval town in Aragon. Getting there in daylight should not have been a problem. However, we made the journey in a similar time to that expected of a dismounted Spanish conquistador in full armour and arrived with only distant memories of the sun.

Even more distant, as it turned out, was the hope of finding somewhere to stay. After two hours of tramping the streets, it became clear that everywhere was booked up and had been for months. Worse still, a light blizzard had started to blow, with the temperature dropping at a rate worryingly consistent with the mood of my family.

As ever, alert to the slightest change in my wife's emotions, I could see that my chances of a gentle night of spontaneous romance were dwindling. Indeed, a few throw-away comments from her seemed to imply that some fast thinking was required if I was to avoid castration before the sun rose again. It was possible that she was less fraught than I thought, but long experience has made me extremely wary.

It is at times like this that even a romantic has to be willing to change his world view. And quickly. Finding God can be helpful and a few prayers never go amiss. However, more immediately useful is cloying obsequiousness, a working mobile phone and sheer good luck.

By chance, a Spanish friend of ours lives in a very small town house in a village close to Albarracín. Ringing him up, I reminded him of how the British had helped Spain during the Napoleonic Wars and said that it was now pay-back time, as my family was in desperate straits. Obviously, I claimed that this was due to my wife absent-mindedly forgetting to book somewhere in advance.

In no time at all, the children were in sleeping bags on our friend's sitting room floor with my wife and I contorted within a minute storage room. Whilst this was something of a success, not even the writer of the Kama Sutra could have envisaged a workable sexual position, let alone have engendered romantic feelings in my wife.

During a brief ceasefire over who should have the only pillow, I tried to enthuse about the romance of the open road, but this fell upon ground as stony as that upon which we lay. Indeed, it seems that if I want spontaneous romance in the future, then it has to be booked well in advance and involve a five star Parador.

A Lesson in Spanish

My sperm count," pronounced Pablo gravely, above the noise of the bar, "is unusually high. For the season."

"Time of year," I corrected automatically, before the full import of his statement had properly sunk in.

"For the time of the year," Pablo corrected himself, "my sperm count is…" he paused, clearly trying to recall a newly learnt word, "remarkable."

"Remarkable," I heard myself mutter, appalled.

Pablo's beautiful, young wife looked at him with loving approval and smiled serenely, hopefully not understanding a word he had just uttered. This was more than could be said for the rest of the class, who had suddenly become extremely attentive.

"Is your sperm count also… remarkable… at this minute?" asked Pablo, turning to me.

I noticed that the rest of the class were craning their necks to scrutinise me, clearly fascinated by this extraordinary digression on the English usage of timings. Paloma, a middle aged housewife, looked at me expectantly whilst Maria, a pretty eighteen year old student, had raised a slightly quizzical eyebrow. Meanwhile, Juan José, a middle ranking executive with a pot belly, had stopped taking notes, to peer at me over his spectacles.

"Well…" I started, squirming in embarrassment. "Can anyone… er… tell me what is… wrong… with what Pablo has just said?"

"Is not possible to know your sperm count at this minute?" suggested Maria, haltingly, mis-understanding me completely.

"Is correct." Paloma confirmed immediately, with maternal authority. "Is impossible."

"Actually, that's not…" I began, weakly, fast feeling that I was losing any semblance of control.

"Is possible you know today, your sperm count, yesterday," growled Juan José in a deep, ponderous and unstoppable baritone. Leaning forward, he adjusted his glasses and glanced at his notes. "Yes. But, no is possible to know sperm count now. This minute. Sitting here in bar."

Inwardly shuddering, I glanced at a crestfallen Pablo, wondering how matters could possibly get worse. Clearly, standing in for my wife to give her weekly English conversational class was a good deal more challenging than I had possibly imagined.

"Actually, in English we don't say: 'at this minute'," I said, desperately trying to steer the conversation away from sperm counts, "instead, we say…"

"So," Pablo suddenly interrupted, with great determination, "was remarkable, your sperm count, yesterday?"

"Well... er..."

"Please." asked Pablo's wife, in a low and hesitant voice.

"Yes, Juanita?" I said, sighing with relief, whilst signalling for the class to allow her, the weakest English speaker, to contribute. "Do go ahead. It can sometimes be very difficult to understand the English use of timings: at the moment, now, in a minute, later, straightaway, instantly and so on. I quite understand. How can I help?"

Juanita looked at me shyly through slightly lowered, deep almond eyes. "Thank you," she said, demurely. There was an expectant silence for a moment, as she braced herself to talk. "What," she began, so softly that I had to stretch forward to hear her, "means..."

"At the moment?" I suggested, helpfully, to encourage her. "In a thrice? At a later date? Some other time? In the future? The distant past? How time flies?"

"Sperm count?" she said, smiling modestly, pleased with her own bravery. "What means: sperm count?"

Oh, my God Fathers! Slumping back into my seat, I could only imagine what my wife was going to say, once the content of the lesson became open knowledge. And how on earth was I going to explain what 'sperm count' was, particularly to the virginal looking Juanita? As it was, I was getting odd glances from people standing at the bar, who had become unusually quiet and seemed to be concentrating, increasingly, on the class. A burst of rapid Spanish from Paloma brought me swiftly back to reality. However, worryingly, it also produced a series of grunts of approval and nodding heads from the on-lookers.

"I explain to Juanita, everything," announced Paloma.

"Splendid," I managed, turning over the page of my wife's text book, in an attempt to move swiftly onto the safer ground of superlatives. Following my lead, the class shuffled their papers.

"Now, let's see what we can do with these." I suggested. "Superlatives tend to form an integral part of most conversations. Who would like to begin?"

"I have," Pablo began, immediately, "the biggest…"

"Thank you, Pablo. *Thank you,*" I interrupted quickly, unnerved by his lack of any taboos and suspecting the very worst. Behind me, the bar had become totally silent and I could feel sweat appearing on my brow. "Quite excellent."

"…a *remarkably* big, an *enormous…*" continued Pablo remorselessly. "…a *huge…*"

"Well," I said, standing up. "That is all we have time for today. Good effort, indeed." Mopping my forehead, I began to walk away, swearing never, ever, again to take another class…

Nick Snelling

A Deserted Place

It would seem that I am to gardens what DDT is to mosquitoes. No sooner do I have a garden than everything within it dies. Either that, or the absolute reverse occurs and I find myself the owner of a jungle so impenetrable that it would drive a determined Amazonian Indian demented.

It is not that I dislike gardens. On the contrary, few things give me greater pleasure. To walk though a beautifully manicured area of scented plants and flowering shrubs, complemented by artfully placed trees and ingenious water features is always a joy. Indeed, few people admire the mystery of a garden that remains colourful, productive and welcoming during the changing seasons, more than me.

The trouble is that at Casa Desolada the gap between admiration and reality is a wide one. Part of the problem lies with my morale, which is still low after years of fruitless, in every sense of the word, gardening in the UK. Indeed, I still bear the mental scars left from mowing two very large lawns virtually throughout the year. All, incidentally, with the aid of a temperamental mowing machine that unnervingly varied its speed, seemingly according to whim, from a despairing child's crawl to a g-force inducing sprint.

If battling with a wilful mowing machine was not bad enough, there was always the vegetable patch with which to contend. This malign patch of ground was an endless disappointment that, despite its considerable size, yielded less sustenance than a small window box hanging from a London bed-sit. Indeed, after several years, it became obvious that it would have been more energy efficient to have eaten the cardboard surrounding the bags of new seeds intended for the garden, than actually planting the contents.

Margaret Dennant

Worse still, there was the endless dilemma of what to do with the wildlife. On the rare occasions that any vegetable emerged nervously from the vegetable patch, it was promptly eaten by some passing rabbit. As a parent, of course, I was expected to be amused by the antics of these cuddly 'bunnys'. As a gardener, however, my response was more conventional and driven by an emotion that Stalin would have recognised instantly.

Sadly, the only time that I decided to exact ultimate retribution, the consequences far outweighed any possible benefits. Borrowing a shotgun from my father, I one day cunningly planted some carrots, bought from the local greengrocer, in the vegetable patch and then awaited the arrival of the first rabbit. Having watched far too many war films, as inaccurate, as it turned out, as my shooting, I chose as my hide a small bathroom overlooking our rear garden.

I did not have long to wait before a rabbit appeared, looking suitably impressed by the newly planted, and unusually delicious looking, carrots. Taking aim, I squeezed the trigger of the shotgun. In the constricted space of the tiny bathroom, the tremendous explosion of the shotgun mimicked that more normally associated with a very large artillery piece. Stunned, totally deafened and shaking like a tuning fork, I was appalled to see that I had hit our neighbour's beloved plum tree, a branch of which had then shattered the door of their greenhouse. Needless to say, the rabbit remained completely unscathed and continued his feast with an astonishing display of sang-froid.

To some extent, this episode hastened our departure from the UK, which was notable for the lack of obvious regret at our leaving displayed by our neighbours. Perhaps still a little upset about the plum tree, they fervently approved of our decision to move to Spain permanently, whilst implying that we should seriously consider a property with a low maintenance garden and absolutely no close neighbours.

At Casa Desolada, our garden is certainly low maintenance. Thankfully, the Spanish climate lends itself to gravelled gardens and tiled terraces surrounding an azure pool. Any plants tend to be restricted to large clay pots leaning at odd angles throughout the garden as though placed there by mistake. This is my type of gardening.

With only distant memories of days mowing lawns, I now enjoy relaxing in my garden. No longer a slave to nettles and weeds and rampaging grass, I have time to sit entertaining friends, whilst watching the changing colours of the beautiful mountain landscape as the day progresses. My irrigation system looks after the plants that need water and anything not irrigated simply does not survive long enough to be a problem. Finally, and joyfully, I have a garden that I can control and one that even an Amazonian Indian would find tempting.

Quite A Gas

Generally speaking, I know exactly what has happened when I hear a high pitched shriek at Casa Desolada, followed by a torrent of furious curses. All coming, invariably, either from the bathroom or kitchen. Without doubt, the gas bottle to the shower or cooker has just run out. Worse still, as the curses become louder and a great deal more personal, it becomes horribly apparent that I have forgotten to refill our spare gas bottles.

Ducking behind the nearest palm tree, my instant reaction, honed by years of marriage, is to take cover and make my way quickly to the car. This I always keep on the roadside and pointing downhill, for just such an emergency. I need only to slide into the driver's seat and ease off the handbrake to make a silent and impressively rapid escape. This is one of the few advantages to living on a mountainside, with this strategic positioning of the car one of the only positive aspects to Casa Desolada.

Certainly, I fully understand the principles behind the 'fight or flight' reaction of the human body when confronted by fear. However, long ago my 'fight' option seems to have disappeared altogether. In many ways, this is a very good thing indeed. It negates any possibility of making the wrong choice and allows all my energies to be concentrated solely upon the 'flight' bit. This is vital, as my wife is nothing if not a daunting adversary and can produce a remarkable turn of speed when provoked.

And when it comes to provocation there are few things that make my wife more incandescently livid than the gas bottle running out, just as she is half way through cooking dinner. Unfortunately, another one of the 'few things' is when the other

Margaret Denmark

gas bottle empties, whilst she is showering - initiating a heart attack inducing, instantaneous drop in water temperature.

This tends to occur to her with an uncanny frequency. Taking a shower, she claims with some justification, is a nerve wracking experience, not unlike a game of Russian Roulette; albeit using a pistol with only two chambers.

Much of the trouble can be placed firmly at the door of my teenage daughter who has an extraordinary capacity to stay in the shower for extended periods. In fact, each time she emerges from the bathroom, I am amazed that she is still much the same size and has not dissolved altogether. Certainly, the quantity of gas she uses is incredible and, probably, equates to the annual output of a medium sized rig in the North Sea.

Perhaps the most extraordinary thing is that a gas bottle has never been known to run out whilst my daughter is in the shower. With uncanny prescience, she seems able to gauge exactly the amount of gas left in the cylinder. This is always just sufficient to bring the shower up to a luxuriously warm temperature for the next person. Lulled into an absurdly false sense of security, they have enough time to fully lather their hair before the water suddenly turns breathtakingly icy.

Unfortunately, for reasons that escape me, females tend to close ranks when things go wrong and divert their extraordinary resources of vitriol to the nearest male, irrespective of the objective facts. Blue lipped, wild eyed and with hair like a Vivienne Westwood designed Gorgon, my wife will appear on our balcony to direct my daughter in a determined hunt for me. The chase is quickly on, with youth battling desperation, as I try to avoid detection whilst frantically attempting to disappear.

My theory, of course, is based upon a time-honoured principle. If I can avoid the initial, concussive effect of my wife's fury then, given sufficient time, her natural good humour will reassert itself as the offending trauma is forgotten. However, like most theories, this tactic rarely works in practice. Getting away cleanly is unusual and the timing of my return nothing if not hazardous.

Certainly, coming back too soon if there were no spare, full gas bottles, can mean entering a maelstrom, with my wife furiously trying to clear her hair of lather, whilst bent over a kettle-filled bowl of water. Returning too late, evidently, indicates malice aforethought, with the emptying of the gas bottle a deliberate act expressly intended to make her late, her hair a mess, sabotage her shopping trip or embarrass her in front of her friends.

Living with gas bottles is not easy. In fact, I suspect that these malign objects are the catalyst for most divorces in Spain and were designed specifically by lawyers to ensure that business remains brisk. Without doubt, orange has become my least favourite colour and one now guaranteed to send shivers up my spine and a hunted look to my face

Porn To Kill

D ios mio!" gasped an ancient widow dressed in a black, square-lady dress squinting disbelievingly down at the DVD box that had just slid to her feet.

"*Oh my God!*" hissed my wife, blushing bright red. Around us the rest of the cafe had gone completely silent, the normal roaring hubub of almuerzo disappearing as fast as my local reputation

On the plus side, the door to the cafe was propped open, my car was within sprinting distance, and I still had some credit on my Barclaycard. Probably only sufficient to get me a place crewing some decrepit iron ore lug to Morrocco but I was in no position to dismiss any potential escape route.

"Es tuyo?" a croaky voice asked, just as I was about to spring for the door.

Reluctantly turning round, I noticed that old Vicente had limped over to me. In his gnarled hand was the DVD – the front cover graphically portraying several naked couples in positions that went well beyond 'compromising'. Indeed, if I had ever had any doubts about what the 'hard' part of hard core pornography meant, then the DVD cover certainly provided all the clarification needed.

"Thank you, Vicente," I managed, gallantly, my mind whirring, "but I think it's my wife's."

To some extent, this was credible. After all she had been the one struggling to open the mysteriously well wrapped, heavily sealed, brown envelope that we had just collected from the post office. She, it had been who had asked for a pair of scissors from the cafe owners and it was from her hands that the DVD box had leapt across the floor, as it was finally

hauled out of the package. How were the villagers to know that it had been addressed to me?

With an astonishingly salacious grin, Vicente creakingly bent towards my wife and handed her the DVD. Frozen to the spot and appalled, my wife was forced to accept a lascivious pat on the cheek and a suspiciously forward wink from the old man, whilst looking at me through narrowed eyes that did not bode well for the future. Certainly, some of her phraseology, as we drove home, could probably have been fitted seamlessly onto the DVD.

After a couple of days, life had returned pretty much to normal. Indeed, several times I was briefly allowed into the house. However, this was not to last long. Unfortunately, my wife took a call on my mobile whilst it was charging on the kitchen worksurface. The call was from a lady lawyer friend who advised my wife, laughingly, that I had been 'seen'.

"Seen?" my wife had asked, "*Seen*?"

"At Cisne's," the lawyer had replied. "You know, the brothel just off the N332. Someone saw Nick there. Everyone's talking about it. "

Indeed. Just about everyone that I met. All of whom refused to believe that I had been commissioned to write an article on prostitution and the sex industry in Spain. And all of whom refused to aknowledge that, in the best interests of research, I had needed to actually interview people in the industry. In fact, of course, it was not the interviews and research that were the problem so much as the irrisistible temptations that were supposedly on offer.

The funny thing is that, like most 'sexy' industries, any glamour is normally wafer thin and the temptations just as illusory. However, when it comes to brothels, no-one can be persuaded otherwise and no-one will believe, in my particular case, that I was not granted the orgy of everyone's dreams – and, better still, 'on the house'. Sadly, I have to report, this did not occur.

Nonetheless, I now seem to have gained something of a reputation in our local community, albeit a rather odd one, that I am quite enjoying. To the men, I am blessed with a sensationally sexy, free-thinking and liberal wife – whilst to the women I am clearly a person of some fascinating notoriety.

Meanwhile, I may still have the last laugh. Someone clearly had 'seen' me at the brothel – in which case he must have been there. Not just that but, as I conducted my interviews beside the lifts to the 'first floor', he must have passed me by. So, his 'research' must have been a good deal more in-depth than mine. I wonder who it might have been? Not another journalist, surely.

A Meter Out

On the rare moments when I have doubts about why I am living in Spain, I am immediately reassured when I drive into my local town of Gandia. Actually, it is not the driving that charms me but the parking.

In Britain, I am used to exercising the greatest caution when parking my car. Indeed, the whole process requires an attention to detail that would unnerve a bomb disposal expert. On the rare occasions that I find a parking place, I know that I have to park strictly within the white lines, with no more than an exact 150mm between the pavement and the wheels. Heaven help me, if my car minutely overhangs the designated area. This is sufficient for a severe and immediate clamping and a fine big enough to threaten the perilous finances of Casa Desolada.

And then, of course, there is the ever-present threat of being towed away for the smallest infringement. A few minutes past the nominated time on a meter and my car will be towed away with a speed and efficiency which, if applied to genuine criminals, would probably eliminate all crime from the UK within days.

The justification for the draconian parking laws in the UK is that we have simply too many vehicles for too small a country. Whilst there may be some truth in this, the reality is that most of the traffic in Britain is composed of clamping vans, tow-away trucks and the countless vehicles transporting traffic wardens to work and back. To make matters worse, further appalling congestion is caused by the myriad of state officials employed in erecting, dismantling and maintaining the thousands of traffic cameras that line our roads. It is all a cunning self-perpetuating

Margaret Denmark

cycle with the main aim, I reckon, to keep the unemployment figures down and tax revenues up.

Matters are very different in Spain where everyone parks where they want, how they want and when they want, with a complete and wonderful disregard for road markings. Here, you are a complete wimp unless you double park on a zebra crossing or leave your car half on a pavement and just below some traffic lights opposite the A and E department of a major hospital. Clamping is virtually unknown and tow-away trucks are objects of real curiosity.

The other day, with a gathering crowd of some thirty people, I had the almost unique experience of actually seeing a car towed away. There was a positively festive atmosphere, with a growing number of Guardia Civil attempting to control the increasingly chaotic operation whilst blowing frantically on their whistles. Quickly all movement, in every direction, came to a halt as traffic backed up and people left their own cars to witness this astounding event. Within ten minutes the whole of Gandia had virtually come to a standstill with an ever-expanding radius of related traffic jams affecting the entire province.

The main topic of conversation around me centred on an avid curiosity about what the driver must have done to suffer the supreme savagery of having his car towed away. Was he an axe murderer, a dangerous bank robber or a child snatcher? Or perhaps, more likely, had he been caught sleeping with the police chief's wife? For sure, he must have done something truly heinous.

I am also delighted to be living in a country where traffic cameras are almost unknown. With some 6,000 in the UK, it amazes me why anyone should have designs about featuring on Big Brother. In Britain, you are already a daily participant in a veritable road movie, with the chances of true stardom pretty good. A small mistake and you can find yourself featured on some TV programme slyly claiming to show us all how to drive better.

I cannot believe that the Spanish, let alone the canny Valencians, will go for traffic cameras in a big way. It is all very well having the opportunity of a brief stardom but it is not always desirable, as a friend of mine found out to his cost. He was caught 'inflagrente delicto' with another woman. Unfortunately, his wife saw the traffic camera picture first when it came through the post, and proved to be even less impressed with his claims of innocence than the police. Whilst my friend's pleas for clemency went down surprisingly well with the courts, his wife's vengeance, on the other hand, was truly wondrous to behold and a sharp lesson to us all.

I only wish that I could park with the cavalier gusto of my Valencian friends. When I can, I shall know that I have fully integrated. Until then I shall be looked upon as just another curious alien spending a pathetically inordinate amount of time and effort trying to find exactly the right, perfectly legal spot to park my car.

A Mistaken Appearance

I pride myself on having very few phobias. However, living in Spain has given me one and, for a writer, a rather disastrous one too.

The problem is the word 'because'. A somewhat superfluous word, you may think, that could be dispensed with easily. However, it is actually one of those irritatingly important words that cements sentences together. To avoid it involves contortions that go well beyond an ageing brain that is already overstretched from its pitiful grappling with the Spanish language.

My phobia is unfortunately restricted to the English language version of 'because' and is entirely due to a few brief appearances, to the common relief of the viewers, on Spanish television. During possibly the shortest media career on record, I confirmed the worst expectations of people who thought that the production standards of Spanish television could not possibly be lowered.

For a while, a couple of years ago, I co-presented a bi-lingual programme on life in our area. This was principally aimed at British ex-pat viewers and any local Spanish who wanted to improve their English. It was also, no doubt, a desperate attempt by the owners of the television station to fill airtime the cheapest way possible.

As a rank amateur, one afternoon I found myself in a television studio interviewing a guest who was only minimally less nervous than myself. Halfway through the interview, I noticed my guest starting to giggle. I was somewhat perplexed by this, but equally rather pleased at the wit that I was so successfully introducing into the annual fruiting cycle of some obscure palm tree.

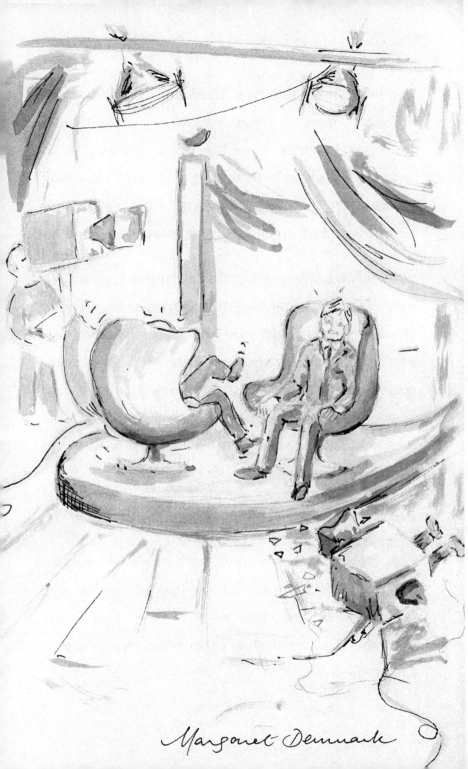

Margaret Denmark

My self-satisfaction was short lived as my guest suddenly gave a final scream of delight and collapsed laughing onto the floor, just as a loud bang reverberated around the studio. Looking round, I saw that one of the cameras had fallen over notwithstanding an heroic effort from its operator.

Somewhat unhinged by this disruption, I waited helplessly for some twenty minutes whilst a new camera was brought into the studio and set up. Finally, the director strode into the studio and, after several linguistic misunderstandings, I gathered that I had to continue the interview after 'because'. This was evidently the last word I had uttered prior to the demise of camera number two.

Because… *BECAUSE*? Because what?

Can you remember a conversation twenty minutes ago during which you said 'because' at some stage? Perhaps you can, but what was it that came beforehand and what on earth were you going to say afterwards?

Before I could fully take into account the enormity of the disaster facing me, I was once again facing camera number two with the operator counting me down. A taped recording of my voice suddenly echoed around the studio: "and, of course, because…"

That was all.

No clues whatsoever. Any chance of knowing what I had been saying beforehand had vanished. I heard myself talking, but the startled eyes of the flowering palm expert said it all…

My last and only hope that the studio would edit the interview prior to broadcast was dashed when I realised that none of them spoke any English and therefore had no idea of the lack of continuity. My desperate pleading that a re-run of the interview was necessary was tragically dismissed as the prima donna attitude of the newly famous. Or, in my case, the seemingly very perverted.

It took me months to live down the hilarity of the local British community who were treated to a lack of continuity that verged somewhere between obscene and utterly revolting. Even now, I meet the occasional Spaniard who is curious as to what we British really do with the inner leaves of a flowering palm.

So, if you meet a Spaniard with a curious usage of 'because' and who starts to talk to you about flowering palms, remember me and, if you are wise, claim a different nationality and back carefully away.

Animal Instinct

One of the things that makes us Britons different from other races is our love of animals. This is curious, as much of what else sets us apart is often not so obviously loveable.

I suspect that the Spanish view us Britons as only slightly toned down versions of the ancient Vikings. We seem to like nothing better than rampaging drinking sessions followed by pointless brawls and the bedding of the nearest female able to stoically withstand our boggle-eyed attentions. Most of us have ambitions of ruling the world again and consider our recent empire as merely a rather feeble first attempt at world domination.

Loving other peoples and their cultures, in short, has never been high on the list of favourable British personality traits. But animals are another thing altogether. So much so, that I cannot believe our fleets were not faced by the Spanish brandishing cuddly rabbits, sad looking donkeys and an array of dogs looking for a good home. This would have disabled our ferocious sailors and left them a cooing mass deserting the field of battle to take their new pets safely home.

At Casa Desolada we are, in some ways, the archetypal British family. Certainly I do tend to blunder around the house after a few drinks and last Saturday night I had a ferocious scrap with a palm tree, having mistaken it for a knife wielding samurai. The only major difference is that my wife is far from stoical about my dismal lovemaking and treats my fumblings with a most disconcerting contempt.

But no matter. Animals we have in profusion, the latest addition to which is a huge Alsatian bitch found deserted on a nearby roadside. This was sufficient for my wife and children to insist that she

was immediately taken into the rather dubious care of our household. For once, I relented in my refusal to have any further pets, as the Alsatian appeared to be exactly what I wanted.

For many years I have hankered after a ferocious guard dog that was totally loyal and protective. You know the sort of thing: a snarling, hackles-permanently-up monster that never leaves your side and is ready to attack anyone at a moment's notice. This has always appealed to what little machismo I still retain and was sure to ward off any unwelcome strangers.

Not that Casa Desolada is blessed with many visitors. Few people willingly enter the premises more than once and those that do are normally eternally bemused social workers or over-excitable psychiatrists. The latter seem to have an insatiable curiosity about my wife's mental stability after twenty years of marriage. I can see where they are coming from, but I keep having nagging doubts about which one of us they believe is bonkers.

Certainly, our Alsatian is as contrary as the rest of the family and has been nothing if not a gigantic disappointment as a guard dog. Indeed, I have encountered more aggressive jelly babies. Yet again, we have had to rely upon the intermittent grunts of my teenage son to ward off any burglars. So far, this has been remarkably successful. Clearly, any potential robbers seem to have come to the same frightening conclusion as my wife and I; that something not quite Homo Sapien exists in our house and that it is rarely safe to enter.

I can just about deal with our Alsatian being non-aggressive. However, what I find less easy to withstand is her insistence upon waking me up in the morning by slobbering all over me. This ghastly ritual makes any alarm clock completely redundant and the prospect of ever having a decent lie-in unthinkable. I have toyed with the idea of buying an automatic feeder and sticking the Alsatian in a kennel. However, this is dangerous thinking for any married man. Given the option, I have more than a sneaking suspicion that my wife would have me at the bottom of the garden and the dog in the house.

Perhaps this explains the drinking binges, global ambitions and erratic behaviour of the average British man. What the Spanish simply do not appreciate is the narrow line we tread. At any moment, we are quite likely to be exchanged in our family's affections by our seemingly far more loveable pets.

A Vine Too Far

Rather good, I think," commented Alberto.

"Excellent," I replied, inadequately, searching for an appropriate term that would least show the depths of my ignorance. "Fruity."

"Fruity?" enquired Sebas, taken aback.

"Fruity," I repeated. "In a friendly, dryish, smooth, sort of way."

Sebas picked up the half empty bottle and peered at it closely. "Could be the wrong label, I suppose," he muttered, delicately sniffing the cork that lay on the cask beside him.

"With," I continued unwisely, to break the silence, "a rich, tempting and curvaceous body."

"Very… seductive." I smiled, warming to my own erudition. "Pleasantly coquettish. Frisky, even."

Sebas looked at me balefully, before turning back to Alberto. "I have left this one until last," he said. "Matured for ten years, from our finest, select vines." With a flourish, a bottle appeared in his hands.

"Oh, my God. Not another one," I thought, glancing at Alberto pleadingly, but I noticed only a suspicious twinkle in his eyes, as he scrutinised the bottle with over-professional care.

"This," enunciated Sebas, like a priest giving a benediction, "is special."

"Special," I said, as approvingly as I could, mistakenly using a word that is awkward to pronounce crisply at the best of times. "Special." For some reason, it still did not sound quite right, with the 'c' sounding ominously slurred. With blurred eyes, I fixed Sebas with my most serious and business-like expression. "Very… Good."

Margaret Denmark

"Amazing bouquet, Sebas," Alberto said, taking a thoughtful sip of the wine, whilst surveying the middle distance, as though concentrating upon an impossibly difficult mathematical problem.

"Bouquet," I heard myself echo unconvincingly, as I looked around vainly, yet again, for a spittoon or at least some receptacle that would take the contents of my glass. But within the rows of immaculately racked oak casks there was not so much as a plant pot to be seen.

Surely, at a wine tasting, it was not usual to fill the glasses nearly to the brim, let alone have to drink the entire contents before trying the next bottle? And, surely, it was not done to taste wine at eleven o'clock in the morning on an empty stomach? Taking a deep breath and mentally crossing myself, I swallowed the contents of the 'special' wine, aware that I was only minutes away from catastrophically subsiding into unconsciousness.

"So, what do you reckon?" asked Alberto, a few minutes later, as we drove away from the vineyard.

"I think, I am beyond thinking," I groaned, trying to bring Alberto into focus but only succeeding in turning his profile into a wavering duplication. "All rational thought left me an hour ago."

It took me two whole days to recover from our wine tasting and a further day before I had the courage to ring Alberto. After all, our trip had been a serious one, with a view to exporting some of Sebas' wine. I was more than a little concerned that I might have blown my cover as an experienced British wine merchant and connoisseur of Spanish regional grapes. From the start, this had seemed a dangerous tactic, as I have difficulty, frankly, distinguishing between a decent Rioja and a bottle of Lea and Perrins sauce.

"It went well," Alberto pronounced confidently. "But it was lucky that, beforehand, I had told Sebas you suffered from a dreadful lisp and always mixed up your Spanish words. Which you do, incidentally."

"But," I asked, ignoring this insult to my hard-learned Spanish, "it cannot be normal to drink so much? I thought wine tasting was about sipping small amounts and tipping the rest away, not downing entire bottles, one after another?"

"Well, this is true. But you are British."

I waited for Alberto to continue but there was only silence at the end of the telephone. Finally, I was forced to ask: "And…?"

"And, Sebas thought, like your compatriots, your rating of the wine would entirely depend upon how drunk you were when you left."

"But I can't remember what I drank."

"Really?" asked Alberto, surprised. "Nothing at all?"

"No, of course not."

"But you liked what you can't remember? After all, you drank a lot of it."

"I suppose I must have done."

I heard Alberto breathe a sigh of relief. "Well then, this is good news. We can ship anything to the UK, so long as it is cheap enough to allow for drinking huge quantities."

"Oh, dear," I thought, "there is something terribly wrong here." It is definitely back to the day job for me. Occasionally, just occasionally, even *I* can see a disaster before it happens…

Nick Snelling

In The Mire

Sadly, I have a feeling that the Spanish have a sense of humour not dissimilar to our own. Perhaps even better. Indeed, I suspect that I have been the cause of much hilarity, with at least one circle of Valencians dining out at my expense, after a visit to our property.

We moved into Casa Desolada a few days before Christmas some years ago knowing, of course, that the house needed some modernising. In fact, it became quickly apparent that nothing had been done to the property, since the incompetent who had first built it. Probably drug crazed and undoubtedly an escapee from an asylum, I doubt the original builder should have been left unsupervised with a set of Meccano. Certainly, entrusting him to build the house must have been an act of faith, by the land owner, equivalent to leaving a teenager behind the wheel of an Abrams tank on a Saturday morning in the parking lot of Carrefour.

Essentially a collection of odd rooms, under an eccentrically shaped roof, Casa Desolada nonetheless stands, if that is the right word, on a fine plot with beautiful views. Charming, in much the same way as a pleasant but completely illogical hallucination, the property seized our attention as a wonderful 'project'. Somewhere that, with a little work, would become a character home and potentially a great investment. It was also the only place that we could afford.

Having moved in, my first job was to install a modern kitchen, as quickly as possible. This was critical because the existing kitchen was an appalling health hazard and would have been deemed intolerable by the leader of a London squat in Tower Hamlets. To add some urgency, a bundle of relatives had

LIMPIA
TUBOS

Margaret Denmark

arbitrarily announced their imminent arrival to help us celebrate our first Christmas in Spain, under the lunatic delusion that we now owned a luxury villa.

With only days in hand, I began ripping out the old kitchen area and installing new units and a splendid worksurface. All was proceeding well, until I had to plumb in the sink. I was a little disturbed when the lead waste pipe came away in my hand but this quickly changed to utter horror. Indeed, a horror as undiluted as the raw effluent starting to ooze remorselessly up through the floor. Despite hysterical efforts, within minutes the kitchen and lounge were covered in an ever rising, stinking and seemingly unstoppable, tide of sewage.

Clearly, there was a blocked main pipe. But where was it?

Fearing a lethal chemical leak of epic proportions, we were soon surrounded by a gaggle of concerned neighbours noisily offering advice. Mostly, this seemed to relate to the details of a good estate agent should we wish to sell quickly. However, it was not long before spades and picks were generously produced and a communal search for the location of the main waste pipe started. By mid-afternoon a line of erratic, if over-enthusiastic, trenches had been vainly dug making our dream property reminiscent of Passchendale, at its worst.

Eventually we decided to call in the professionals. The following morning an old, barrel-chested Valencian waded his way to us, dragging a long hose connected to his bowser-like lorry. For two hours, we tried desperately in pidgin Spanish to communicate with him. However, infuriatingly, all that we could gather was that his quote reflected his absolute, and clearly totally misplaced, confidence about both finding, and clearing, the still-hidden pipe. Despairingly, I finally agreed to him starting work, expecting a further waste of both time and money.

The old Valencian sniffed the pungent air, looked penetratingly up at the sky, peered at an old olive tree and then, skirting a trench, picked up a crow bar. Walking three steps further, he scratched his head a couple of times before melodramatically plunging the crow bar into the ground. Astoundingly, he hit the pipe precisely and half an hour later had completely cleared years of detrius. It was at this point that an unknown man emerged from the lorry's cab.

"Everything all right?" he said, in near perfect English.

Astounded, I asked him where he had been during our absurdly tortuous negotiations?

"In the cab, of course," he replied. "Listening to you and Pablo. Best fun I've had for ages."

Almost speechless, I asked him about his colleague's remarkable pipe divining abilities?

"Had exactly the same problem, exactly the same place, a couple of years ago."

Of course! And if our positions had been reversed, I doubt I could have resisted the fun on offer either...

Life's A Beach

I cannot be the only person who shudders at the memory of summer holidays spent by the beach in the UK. Indeed, in normal circumstances, I reckon there would be a decent case for national compensation for most of us for physical and emotional distress.

Certainly, few experiences were more distressing than spending two weeks trudging down to an east coast beach every day, to be confronted by twelve hours of icy, battering winds and a savage, foam flecked, green sea. Huddled beside breakwaters, wearing overcoats and yet still blue from the cold, it is amazing that our children reach adulthood or that any parent retains their sanity.

Of course, there are good reasons for the mass summer migration to our beaches although, up until now, this has been kept a closely guarded secret. Laughably, many foreigners think the rash of sand castles covering our summer coastline are an eccentric and desperate attempt by us British to keep warm, whilst reliving the glories of our medieval past. This is a typical misunderstanding and takes no account of the indomitable character of the Anglo Saxon.

In fact, the sand castles are just distractions, vitally important since the end of the Cold War, with the proliferation of enemy spy satellites circling the globe. It is not the castles that are important, of course, but the thousands of holes penetrating deep into the sand beside them.

For many years there has been real concern, at the highest levels, of the probability of another French invasion, this time using dozens of tunnels secretly driven under the Channel. We were taken by

surprise once by the French in 1066. But it is certainly not going to happen again. Not since our wise and far-sighted leaders decided to act, even if it has meant placing patriotic families under appalling privations during the summer holidays.

The plan, sound and supremely cunning, is that as the tide comes in any French tunnel will be instantly detected by our 'sand castle builders' and swamped. Our old enemies will then be repelled before they can charge up onto the sacred soil of Britain.

Meanwhile, thankfully, an ingenious parallel strategy has been initiated that closely involves Spain. Generously supporting cheap flights, successive governments have encouraged vast numbers of elite Britons to settle on the Iberian peninsular. This has been to ensure that a clandestine army was in place and ready, at a moment's notice, to march north to execute a classic pincer movement up into the soft underbelly of France.

Of course, us ex-patriots are under a duty to blend into the Spanish background, whilst determinedly acclimatising ourselves to the very different conditions and rigours of the Mediterranean. Hard though it is, all of us have to concentrate, constantly, upon ridding ourselves of our pale skins and our tell-tale, super fit, British bodies.

At Casa Desolada, I believe that we have responded honourably to the task in hand. Time and again, we have shown an iron determination that would have been proudly recognised by our Empire-building forefathers. Of all people, they would have known how difficult it is to have a daily siesta and then go to the beach to labour away developing a golden tan. Often, it has taken a punishing self-discipline to drink yet another tankard of sangria or request the largest possible postre during a vast menu del dia. However, this we have done and now stand, somewhat unsteadily, it has to be said, ready for our country's rallying call.

Occasionally, our dedication has been exceeded by gallant compatriot friends, who have even taken the bold and unusual step of learning a foreign language. More than once, I have been startled by an approaching Briton saying, almost fluently: "Hola! Como estas?" My only concern has been whether this is a worrying indication of someone 'going native' and dangerously forgetting their divine responsibilities to our mother country.

Certainly, it can be easy to forget the British coast when you are living beside an azure sea in a blissfully benign climate. Indeed, I do wonder whether, when our rallying call comes, there may be a rather poor turnout. Maybe, living here is our compensation and that our fear of the French has been a touch exaggerated. Such a thing is possible, I suppose?

Newton's Balls

L ike most Britons, my family have a strong nomadic streak, with few things giving us greater pleasure than responding to the urgent call of the road. Indeed, it is rare to find the members of Casa Desolada more invigorated and lively than when travelling.

Having said that, 'lively' may not be a description that my wife would necessarily use in the most positive sense of the word. Mainly, this is due to the occasional disagreement that we have relating to navigation.

Like most men, I have a contempt for maps that goes deep into my psyche. My forefathers did not have maps and, like me, relied upon their superb and highly honed sense of direction. In times past, men never got lost, despite criss-crossing an entirely unknown and unmapped world. Boldly going forth across vast oceans, into barely penetrable jungles and through barren deserts, they always found their way home. They did not need maps. There was never a question of being lost, only minor delays, as they worked out the most efficient way of surmounting previously unseen mountain ranges or daunting, ice-encrusted obstacles.

Sadly, my wife's response to man's claims to an almost mystical sense of direction is brutal. She seems to think that the only way man ever found his way home is due to the world being round, thus enabling our forefathers to blunder remorselessly forward until they returned to exactly where they started from. If the world had been flat, my wife claims, there would be a distinct lack of males around. This is laughable, thoroughly inaccurate, and, I fear, invariably said in the heat of the moment just as I am almost on the point of establishing our location.

GRANADA BAZA

Margaret Denmark

Travelling through Spain I have, many times, demonstrated that I can get us home. Given sufficient time. Indeed, more often than not, I have even managed to arrive with my family in pretty much the place we were aiming for. All of this has been achieved notwithstanding the distraction of tearful, hungry children and a monosyllabic wife.

For example, only recently, we successfully popped down to Granada to see the Alhambra. It is true that the trip took a touch longer than intended due to an unplanned excursion. However, as I said to my wife, sometimes it is pleasant to take an unexpected detour and going a different route can be enjoyable. It was certainly disappointing to find the Alhambra locked when we finally found it, but then how was I to know that it would be closed at midnight?

Many times, my wife has pleaded with me to ask for directions, when a subversive uncertainty about where we are has pervaded the car. This I have found particularly hurtful. Did the first astronauts rely upon directions to the moon? Or Meriwether Lewis and Clark ask the way across America during their epic two year expedition? Of course not.

Anyway, who would I ask? Another man? Hardly, that is just not done. A woman, perhaps? Unthinkable! All I would get is a tirade, questioning why I lacked a decent map and had not asked someone for directions before I got lost. Whilst this has a certain unassailable female logic, I would hardly ask directions unless I knew that I was going to get lost in the first place. Thus would start a lengthy philosophical conversation between my wife and our lady 'advisor' that would end up encompassing all man's faults, including why we persist in leaving the loo seat up. Whilst my wife would, no doubt, have gained a lifelong friend, the chances are that the car would have run out of petrol by the time both had finished.

No, it is the joy of perpetual motion for me. In future, I shall only announce our destination when I decide that we are there, wherever 'there' may turn out to be. And that is the answer, really. If you do not know where you are going then you cannot possibly be accused of being lost. It is true that coming back home may prove problematic, but then I might be tempted to prove my wife's odd theory about the world being round. Where she got this idea from, I really do not know. On the rare occasions that I have seen a road map, it has shown the world as flat as a pancake.

In the meantime, we shall continue travelling through Spain's fascinating hinterland. There is much to see and it is amazing how invigorating it is when the rest of the family are unaware that, secretly, I now have a hand-held GPS.

On The Run

At Casa Desolada we are a free thinking family, with views and opinions equally expressed and openly discussed. Our conversations range widely, with the children encouraged to probe issues from international affairs to the influence of classical philosophers on contemporary life. We explore the writings of great authors and meditate upon the merits of differing religious beliefs. We even have heated exchanges about the development of the rule of law, its application to sweet shop access and the awful iniquities of an autocratic justice system. We are nothing, if not liberal.

However, there are two areas upon which discussion is absolutely forbidden. These are taboos that, over a period of time, have taken deep root. The first is anything to do with family finance. This controversial topic has been deemed too horrifying for an open forum. Neither my wife nor I feel that the children are strong enough yet to withstand the night terrors and fits of terrible shaking that occur to us after the arrival of our bank statements. It is one thing for them to debate the dreadful privations of emerging countries, but quite another to hear that the family economy is on a par with that of Zimbabwe.

The second taboo relates to exercise. In the distant past, my wife and I prided ourselves on our fitness. This was demonstrated principally by our membership of numerous gyms and our obsessive purchase of sports clothes. Indeed, few couples have leant against the bar of a fitness club looking more convincing than ourselves. Wearing the finest quality trainers and clutched by Lyrca, no-one could have doubted our commitment to the body beautiful.

Fortunately, the gym owners, at the time, were nothing if not discreet and never let on that the only exercise we accomplished was walking from the car to the bar. My tales of terrifically hard won points whilst playing the best squash player in the club were indulged, so long as our membership fees were paid regularly. Lithe and young, we could get away with sitting convincingly at the bar, whilst blustering about the confusing merits of weight training and step aerobics, kick boxing and dance classes.

However, now matters are very different. The years have taken their toll and have not been helped by our over-indulgent lifestyle in Spain. Too many menus del dia and bottles of fine Rioja have meant that any thoughts of wearing Lyrca again are quickly dismissed. Those days are over, or at least until Lyrca develops sportswear that has the tensile strength of Kevlar matched by the stretching capacity of a weak elastic band.

In hushed tones, well away from the children, we do occasionally act on the pressing requirement to do something about our fitness. Indeed, recently my wife daringly dusted the mothballs from her exercise mattress and placed it in a secluded part of our underbuild. She now does a daily sit-up, which she claims has made an enormous difference. Certainly, it appears effective, although I have a nagging feeling that she is holding her breath in a little more each time she demonstrates her new self to me.

Mind you, the last time that I did *any* exercise, it was when I rather stupidly agreed to play five-a-side football with some youngsters from our village. Dazzlingly fit, and obsessed by the 'beautiful game', the Spanish ran rings around me. My only moment of glory came when I scored my side's only goal. All too predictably, this was due to an alarmingly powerful volley from a defender accidentally rebounding off my rump and rolling past the unsuspecting and thoroughly amazed goalie.

It took me several days to recover from my feeble efforts on the pitch, which rendered me incapable of coordinated thought or movement. Speechless from the aches and pulled muscles, I dragged myself around the house bemoaning my lot, whilst swearing that I would never again allow my body to undergo such appalling and terrible torture.

I am all for freedom of speech and grateful that Spain has become such a demonstration of democracy. However, there are limits and I would rather have Franco back in power than raise the subject of exercise or personal finance in Casa Desolada. There are some things that are simply too terrible to talk about.

Out of Touch

The other afternoon I was lounging dreamily at my desk admiring, through a heat haze, the beautiful Valencian countryside stretching high into the mountains above Casa Desolada. An air of peace and tranquillity had finally descended upon the house and I felt my eyes gently closing in response to the natural, timeless rhythm of siesta.

As my head nodded onto my chest, my mobile telephone rang. Groaning, I knew that I had to answer it. After all, my family were out raiding a new shopping mall and they could have been in danger or, more likely, have triggered some dire retail crisis.

"Just seeing if you were there," said a disembodied voice, "about to send you an e-mail." Before I could utter an expletive, the line went dead. Glowering at my computer, I heard a ping as an in-coming e-mail alert sounded.

Very few matters require an immediate response so, ignoring the e-mail, I snuggled deeper into my chair, allowing the glorious afternoon drowsiness to return. No sooner had my eyes closed, than my mobile rang again.

"Did you get the e-mail?" asked my previous caller, pointlessly, just as my home telephone started ringing. Ping! went my computer, this time with a flashing amber light, indicating an MSN message. With any semblance of a dreamy peace fast disappearing into a maelstrom of chaos, I snatched the telephone from its rest as it started to ring.

"Red or blue?" asked the voice of my wife.

"*Blue*, darling."

Margaret Denmark

"*Darling*?" queried the surprised voice on my mobile telephone, as a whirring and clicking noise started from the end of my desk, with a fax starting to grind its way slowly out of the machine.

"Are you with someone?" she probed, suspiciously.

"Perhaps we should meet up?" continued the voice, suddenly husky, on my mobile, as I juggled with both telephones, whilst trying to double click the mouse on my computer with an elbow. "Somewhere quiet and…"

Disbelievingly, rubbing the unrequited sleep from my eyes, I did what I should have done a long time ago. Turning off both telephones, I went to the spaghetti junction of wires curled around the base of my desk and disconnected them all. As the screen on my computer darkened, blissful silence briefly returned to the house.

And people ask whether communications in Spain are good!

Unfortunately, communications in Spain are as all-encompassing as in the UK. At the last count at Casa Desolada, we had four mobile telephones, one fax line, one landline, four e-mail addresses, as many MSN addresses, Skype and, of course, the post. We also, after much resistance from me, have satellite TV and ADSL to ensure that the piles of absolutely irrelevant messages that we are sent are received at breathtaking speed. In all, our house almost equates to a NASA operations room during an acute emergency. It is astounding that we do not glow in the dark.

Obviously, this is all too much. As a confirmed Luddite, I came to Spain to get away from it all. Instead of which, I reach communications overload several times a week, whilst paying an array of telecom bills that probably amount to the monthly wage of a New York brain surgeon.

The answer, of course, is simple. I need to find a communications 'black hole'. My wife has rather too enthusiastically mentioned that my entering a monastery would be a fine start. However, this would mean leaving my credit cards unmonitored. Whilst it is true to say that their combined worth is no greater than the value of their melted plastic, they still have a sentimental value that I hold dear from more prosperous days.

More to the point, I fear that even monks sworn to monastic silence now have obligatory access to the internet in their cells. Doubtless their prayers are directed to some over-interactive web site such as www.almightyreunited.com. This probably provides them with a battery of reassuring, if somewhat baffling, automatically generated Delivery Status Notifications. No doubt these then create an endless round of noisy, and excited MSN messages between the cells as the monks prepare each other for final instructions from celestial cyber-space.

In reality, I suspect that I am doomed. Satellites cover virtually every inch of the earth and it is practically illegal not to be armed with at least one mobile, even whilst walking in the benign Valencian countryside. Perhaps the best that I can hope for is the passing of some strict legislation that restricts any form of communication during siesta. Now that would be a coup for Spain!

Nick Snelling

In Vino Veritas

Few things show the difference between the British and the Spanish more than their separate approaches to drinking. A few weeks ago, this was encapsulated in a conversation that I had with a British executive of an international company, the morning after a party:

"Good man, that fellow Harris," commented the senior executive, to my surprise. "See him last night?'"

I admitted that I had.

"Never seen the Zulu warrior song done like that before. Really let his hair down – amongst other things! Shame the waiter was knocked out, but Harris was completely plastered, you know."

"I noticed," I said.

"Then he was sick all over the MD's car and had a hell of a row with the Guardia Civil, before four of them carried him off."

I shuddered at the memory.

"Definitely got a great future with the company," the executive continued, enthusiastically. "Lots of uumph and mixes so well. Like a man full of spirit."

He was certainly not lacking in *that* department, I thought. Anymore spirit and he would have evaporated altogether.

Of course, to do Harris justice, in the UK a party is a 'mission'. It is something that must be undertaken with the greatest seriousness and should not be attempted without years of dedicated training. To do otherwise would be to court failure and its accompanying public humiliation. Indeed, no man in Britain ever approaches a forthcoming party without trepidation: his very life will be on the line and any promotion prospects, whether social, sporting or work will be at stake.

Margaret Denmark

A Briton's very manhood hinges upon how much alcohol he can consume, within the short space of a concentrated few hours. Of course, this means drinking vast quantities of liquid, similar to the amounts received by someone desperately undergoing a major blood transfusion following a traumatic accident. Fairly quickly, a transformation will occur that would have deeply impressed even Dr Jekyll himself. The quiet, unpopular, little man in a tank top and pebble spectacles will become a roaring Berserker capable of mind-boggling behaviour. Irrespective of how appalling his conduct, he will prove himself worthy of his peers and will, unsteadily, be approvingly embraced by all.

The Spanish seem to view parties quite differently. Or perhaps their women are more cunning. Not only do they insist on being present at parties, but they bring their children along as well, irrespective of the time of night. Of course, this would be considered intolerable in the UK, where parties are not really places for women and avowedly not for children. This ingenious ploy completely emasculates most men immediately. However hard you try, it is really difficult to get roaring drunk and behave like a three year old having a tantrum, when nearby four year olds are behaving better.

Even more disruptive, in my experience, is the look on a wife's face suggesting that yet another bottle of beer will undoubtedly result in the immediate and irrevocable withdrawal of all marital rights for the foreseeable future. This scary thought is enough to sober most men and is a disciplinary threat equivalent to having to face, alone and unarmed, a battalion of battle-hardened Paras harbouring a grudge. Certainly, no amount of alcohol has ever managed to transform my reserves of courage, when my wife gives me the 'no more conjugals' look.

No, a Spanish party is altogether a different matter, where alcohol plays a very small part in proceedings and where, with the whole family around, the occasion is invariably delightfully peaceful and joyously civilised. That said, I am still not entirely used to seating arrangements where the men occupy one end of a table and the women the other. Like most men, this brings out the worst of my insecurities, as I see a conspiracy of females clearly exchanging the deepest confidences about our inadequacies. And then, giggling hysterically about them.

Completely unnerved, the drive home is always a tentative one, as I learn the previously hidden, and often pretty extraordinary, peccadilloes of my male friends. Engrossing though this is, I fear, despite my wife's earnest protestations, that there has been a worryingly free exchange of information. This can lead to some odd encounters, when I later bump into male friends who had attended the party. Depending upon the indiscretions revealed by our wives, we treat each other with either renewed respect or very considerable wariness.

But, given the choice, I would not now exchange a British party for a Spanish one, even if it means that my deepest secrets tend to be frighteningly open knowledge. In truth, this is a small penance for not suffering crippling hangovers, let alone weeks of placating a furious wife, embarrassed by my lunatic drunken antics. And, of course, after a Spanish party, there is even the possibility of being invited into the matrimonial bed. Now, that really *is* worth something...

Nick Snelling

Small Talk

Of course, there are flaws to living in Spain. Nowhere is totally perfect. Indeed, there is one particular and devastating problem that everyone living here has to face, on a daily basis. So serious is this problem that it can affect any decision to move to Spain permanently. It is a cloud on all our horizons. And yet, this terrible flaw is rarely written about and only ever mentioned in hushed tones amongst the most intimate of friends. Never, under any circumstances, would it be discussed with strangers.

Small talk. That is the problem and it is no laughing matter.

In the UK it is so easy. Indeed, to be considered a great conversationalist endowed with wit, elegant language and a stunning capacity for scintillating repartee is not unusual. Never would you hear of an encounter where two strangers were left desperately looking at each other, squirming in embarrassment, with nothing to say. Such an excruciating experience is impossible to imagine.

By immediately turning to the weather, in the UK you are guaranteed of an appreciative audience. Indeed, 99.9% of all conversations revolve around this fascinating topic. Even world class management courses stress the importance of being able to talk fluently about the weather. Sensibly, they consider it vital that any aspiring senior executive can, at the very least, quickly and coherently front a presentation analysing the probable highs and lows of the coming months.

Look behind the dry minutes of an ICI board meeting and you will find nothing more than endless debates about the pressures of the coming week. The same is true of the cabinet, where it

would be unthinkable for a new minister to interrupt the PM, as he was charismatically killing time by discussing the frosty nature of trans-Atlantic relations or stormy prospects for the economy.

"How was the weather for you, darling?" is a tender refrain, frequently heard between lovers and the newly married late at night in the UK. When temperatures have been raised, it is exactly this type of caring small talk that can mean so much. It is the very lightning conductor of sound relationships. Without small talk, the days can be very dull indeed.

Tragically, in Spain, the weather rarely changes from one day to the next. There is only sun under an azure sky, day after day. Understandably, this can bring on deep depressions. Spain's wonderful climate simply eliminates the traditional sources of small talk. Recently, for example, I overheard a typical conversation between a local Briton living in my village and a recently arrived British tourist:

"Hello," said the tourist.

"Hello," replied the local, suspiciously.

"Lovely weather!"

After a long pause, "Yes," stated the local.

"Looks good for tomorrow?" suggested the tourist.

There was a pregnant silence, whilst the local shuffled his feet and stared up into the sky, clearly desperately searching for inspiration. Finally, agonisingly, he replied: "Yes." Perplexed, and with an injured look of rejection, the tourist nodded politely and moved on.

In the bar, some minutes later, I happened to see the local who was explaining to a friend how he had just met a charming visitor. However, he had been totally unable to strike up a meaningful conversation. Looking misty-eyed, he commented on how easy it would have been in the UK. "It's such a breeze over there," he commented, "but here…"

Of course, we need to develop a new tactic. Whether we like it or not, we have to get to grips with small talk, whilst finding a reliable topic that will be instantly attractive to any newly met person. After all, the Spanish seem to chat away happily to whoever they meet and I cannot believe that their small talk is about the weather. More probably, it is about their obsession with football, which would prove that every cloud has a silver lining and, in this case, a wonderful topic of instant interest to all.

Unless, of course, you have no interest in the 'beautiful game'. But that would be unthinkable, if you are living in Spain, and definitely not something to voice to a stranger. It would result, I fear, in another unsettling silence. So, if you loathe football, the choices are simple: become a reluctant addict, retreat into embarrassed silence or return to the UK and suffer the weather. I know what I have chosen…

That Sinking Feeling

Without doubt, to have one's own swimming pool is the ambition of anyone coming to live in Spain, with the benighted occupants of Casa Desolada, originally, being no exception to this rule. I say 'originally' as having a pool has stretched our normal equilibrium beyond its limits.

The problem, of course, has been down to chemicals or, in my case, a complete and utter lack of understanding of them. Indeed, the last few years have confirmed what my teachers at junior school seemed to know instinctively: that any form of science or technology was always going to be completely beyond me.

Never before has a swimming pool been assaulted so incompetently, nor changed colours so rapidly, from a turgid green one day through to a noxious pink the next. On the rare occasions our pool has appeared clear and blue, it has been the cause of a stunned and disappointingly short lived celebration. About as short lived, frankly, as anyone brave enough to attempt swimming in a cauldron of unstable and highly toxic chemicals.

On a scorching day recently, a visitor tragically mistook my family's reluctance to enter our pool first, for good manners. With a courage that was breathtaking, in every sense of the word, our friend impetuously leapt into our pool in a doomed attempt to cool down. Brief seconds later, he erupted out of the water like an uncoiled spring, both hands clutching his nether regions, his eyes bulging manically.

Margaret Denmark

"Still far too much chlorine," my daughter commented, knowledgably, just before our visitor let out a terrific, and disturbingly high pitched, shriek.

Whilst my family looked upon the wild gyrations of our friend with some equanimity, the same could not be said of our Spanish neighbour. A woman of a certain age, she has a habit of turning up at the most inopportune moments. Seeing our visitor savagely hurl his chemically impregnated trunks into the olive trees was clearly a shock. However, to then watch him publicly massaging copious amounts of sun oil onto his private parts, whilst moaning loudly, clearly confirmed her worst suspicions of the British. Worryingly, I saw her expression range from deep, Catholic offence to a fleeting but rather unnerving salaciousness.

I fear the pool must go before it is also, rightfully, designated as a major health hazard by the authorities. As it is, our frequent trips to the local surgery have already created some alarm within the village.

The last time we went to the local doctors' surgery there was a rush to the exit from all but the most severely crippled patients. Whilst this saved a good deal of time queueing, it did our popularity little good, as our appearance seemed to revitalise medieval fears of the Great Plague. A slight over-exuberance on my part with some new, all-purpose shock tablets had led to a blotching of our skin so extraordinary as to make a Jackson Pollock painting look pallid by comparison.

My family bore their new appearance in public with surprising good humour and impressed the village enormously with their forbearance, dignity and gently forgiving nature. However, back within the four walls of Casa Desolada matters were very different indeed, with my wife displaying a lack of sympathy for the Human Rights Act that would have impressed a dictator from 1950's Albania. Indeed, I spent a full week living in a stony silence, whilst being placed on a punitive diet of cold lentils and beans.

Ironically my salvation came from our pool which, over the course of the week, had been transformed from the watery equivalent of quick lime to a sublime paradise for breeding mosquitoes. Faced by a delegation of concerned locals, my wife felt compelled, in the finest traditions of community spirit, to allow me a last attempt to make the pool useable.

In fact, the pool now looks in pretty good shape, although this has been largely due to the efforts of our Spanish neighbour, who seems to have developed a far greater ambition than us to see the pool in working order. Whilst this has delighted my family, to my consternation, I have noticed that our neighbour's dress sense has changed. Increasingly, she comes round in clothes that probably came from a 1970's Ann Summers catalogue and only yesterday, unless I misunderstood her, she made a less than oblique comment about sun oil, its many uses and swimwear in trees.

Ambition or no ambition, the pool must definitely go!

Well Salted

At Casa Desolada, we live fifteen minutes from some of the finest beaches in the world. On Gandia playa, golden sand stretches away into the far distance, only interrupted by charming wooden bars, imperious palm trees and a few discrete play areas for children. The sea is always an inviting blue and gently laps along a slight rise in the sand. During the summer, the water reaches bathwater temperature and allows luxurious bathing for hours at a time. It is a Briton's dream.

So, why do we go down to the beach so rarely? Last year, I think we went twice, which, for an ex-pat family with two children, is heresy. I can hardly believe it myself. However, as always, matters at Casa Desolada are never simple.

Certainly, the concept of spontaneously nipping down to the beach is unthinkable. The very thought sends shivers down my spine. For starters, I need time in which to ensure that my physique is up to scratch. Like most men, I believe I have the sculptured body of a Greek God, however occasional bouts of cold reality bring me unpleasantly back to earth.

The other day, for example, I made the mistake of coming out of the shower before our full length mirror had fully steamed up. To my horror, looking back at me was a nightmarish creature closely resembling an upright albino walrus with the legs of a flamingo. Obviously, this was due to a rather dreadful and, I may say, spiteful, distortion in the mirror. However, it was sufficient to dent my confidence and indicate that I was likely to achieve even fewer glances of breathless admiration from surrounding bathers than normal. Clearly, some immediate exercise with my rusting Bullworker was required, with any visit to the beach inconceivable for at least two weeks.

Margaret Denmark

Needless to say, I am not the only member of Casa Desolada who needs to ponder the potentially appalling implications of thoughtlessly rushing down to the beach. My wife will certainly go nowhere near it, until she has a perfect all-over tan. This seems to involve hours of almost mystic concentration, broken only by erratic moves around the garden to seek the perfect combination of sun and shade. Little is heard from her, apart from the occasional high pitched, and very ill-tempered, yelp as delicate parts make contact with one of our less forgiving cacti.

And then, of course, there is the potentially marriage breaking dilemma of swimwear. As the beach day approaches, I find myself forced to make choices that would have given Soloman a nervous breakdown, as my wife tries out a bewildering array of bikinis and swimsuits: high cut, low cut, g-string, padded, underwired, all enveloping, underwhelming, strapless, or crossed over the shoulder. Having come to a design consensus, the computations then spiral into the cosmic impossible as the initial choice is marred by not being patterned, striped, swirly, black, white, green, yellow or whatever happens to be the year's 'in' colour. The whole exhausting process is an agonising shuffle along a tightrope, with divorce lying to one side and a cruel and immediate death to the other.

Finally arriving at the beach, matters are rarely helped by us both having quite different ideas on the perfect place to be. Whilst my wife and I choose our desired location dependent upon who is around, that is the closest we come to any agreement. Strangely, she likes somewhere deserted that is tranquil and devoid of humanity. However, I prefer the hubbub of people. Or, at least, a decent wobble of preening, topless beauties. Not that I mention this, of course, vehemently claiming that being near other people is proof of our determination to integrate. Unfortunately, this cuts no ice at all.

Predictably, we end up miles from anyone until an extended Spanish family settle close by, notwithstanding the acres of barren sand around us. Of course, the last thing we need, after a testing couple of weeks, is half a dozen excitable young children haring around us. All amidst that most lethal and terrifying of combinations to any adult: water and sand.

After having ducked flying balls and an out of control Frisbee and with grit trapped in every possible sun oil encrusted crevice, our retreat home occurs rapidly with vague promises of another outing. But not, of course, too soon.

However heretical, I reckon it is safest for all concerned if we admire the beaches from a safe distance, whilst remaining, bulging, palid and unfashionable around our own pool.

Relative Success

Before the propeller stopped turning, the two Guardia Civil officers were beside the microlight. I had seen them as we glided gently towards the little patch of green runway and I had given them a cheery wave. This had not been reciprocated and I could now see their stony faces promised only trouble. I tried smiling brightly but this only produced a firm hand on my upper arm as I stepped out of the cockpit. Behind me Juan, the pilot, was faring no better.

"Innocent," I announced, rather optimistically, to the Guardia Civil officer holding onto me.

"Illegal runway," he retorted in heavily accented English, as we headed for the police car. Behind me, Juan had started to chat to the officer with him.

"You happen to work with Juan Baptiste?" he asked.

His officer grunted dismissively.

"Used to work with Vicente Raya – the old superintendent at the Fire Station."

"*Ven!*" growled the officer, irritably. "Move it."

"His daughter went to school," continued Juan, undeterred, "with the beautiful Maria José, who married Pablo Escriva, lucky fellow. Works at the Notaire's office…"

"Maria José?" queried the officer with me, letting go of my arm. "Lives in Xeraco?"

"Yes, lovely girl. My father is her God father."

"*You* know Maria José," said the officer, turning to his companion. "The Captain's niece. Drives that blue Audi she parks in the station whenever she goes shopping in Valencia."

Margaret Denmark

"Know her?" asked the officer beside Juan. 'Pablo's my second cousin. Of course, I know her...'

Completely excluded from this conversation, I could see the wonder of Spain working again. By this time, we were standing by the police car with the two officers and Juan suddenly chatting, as if old friends, with any thoughts of arrest long since dispelled. Indeed, within a few minutes the two officers had their pistols out and were extolling the differing benefits of each other's weapons, with Juan trying out the balance of each. Eventually, with a friendly warning and a pat on the back for Juan and a smiling handshake for me, the Guardia Civil left.

The first time that I had seen such a bewilderingly wonderful demonstration of networking, it had occurred at my lawyer's office late on a chilly Saturday night. An important deal that I had negotiated during the week had unravelled uncontrollably. My lawyer, an able lady called Maite, had tried vainly to resurrect the deal with the main contractor on the telephone. It was 10.30pm and we were all feeling tired, disappointed and frayed.

"We are," Maite sighed finally, rubbing the fatigue from her eyes, "getting no-where."

"Indeed," I said, getting up. "I fear it is unworkable."

"I have tried as a lawyer. But now, sadly, if you agree, I can try as a Valenciana?"

I looked curiously at Maite, not understanding what she meant. "Whatever," I answered, walking irritably over to the coffee machine.

"Rosa," Maite called to her assistant, "do you know Pedro Garcia? He lives in Calle Argentinas, in the flats above the new pharmacy?"

"Pedro Garcia? No, but my aunty lives nearby. I could call her."

"Thank you." Maite turned back to me, with a resigned expression in her eyes. "I train for seven years and now I am a lawyer for ten years." In the background I could hear a burst of excitable Valencian from Rosa, as she spoke on the telephone. "And always it is the same thing. You will see."

Over the next half an hour I drank two cups of coffee, whilst peering impatiently into the rain swept darkness outside. In truth, I was waiting as a matter of good manners, rather than through any prospect of success. However, shortly before 11pm, Rosa bustled into Maite's office, smiling. A moment later, the telephone started ringing and Maite picked up the receiver, her face furrowing with concentration.

"You see," she said, putting the telephone down, "everything is now alright. The contract will go ahead, as planned."

"*Really*? No problems?"

Maite shrugged her shoulders and arched her eyebrows expressively. "None. And you know why? Because I am a great lawyer?" Maite shook her head.

"No! Because Pedro's flat is opposite someone called Maria, who is the best friend of a woman who lives on the ground floor. Evidently, the woman on the ground floor works in the new pharmacy and breakfasts daily with Rosa's aunt. Maria told Pedro to stop being so stupid, because he was upsetting Rosa and this was distressing for Rosa's aunt. And, as you know, Rosa does not just work for me, she is the granddaughter of my father's cousin."

I left the office with my head spinning. How very, very different life is here...

Nick Snelling

Where Danger Lurks

I suspect that every country has a danger zone of some kind. For example, in Indonesia there are tsunamis, in America hurricanes, in Iraq bombs, in Australia poisonous spiders and in the UK, well, taxes.

However, these life threatening perils are nothing compared to that found in Spain. Here, I have seen grown men, whose boldness is beyond question, go pale and tremble uncontrollably. I have, myself, often felt a cold trickle of sweat run down between my shoulder blades as a sharp stab of agonising psychosomatic pain has struck deep in the pit of my stomach.

I am no mere wimp. I have seen things and been places. I have nearly looked my bank manager in the eye whilst having a full and somewhat too frank discussion about my overdraft. I have endured a two week summer holiday on the British east coast. Once, I even said a flat no to my teenage daughter and almost kept to it. I have, as they say, been around and seen what horrors life can throw my way.

Hardened and battle scarred, I came to Spain with no fears. There was nothing, so I thought, that could disturb my zen-like equilibrium.

Which just shows how terribly wrong you can be.

Shopping. That is the problem. One simple word with a resonance to men that is more powerful and terrifying than any other found in the English language. If the Gestapo had uttered this one word in the cells of occupied Europe they would have learnt every secret the Allies possessed. No man can withstand brooding too long on 'shopping' without his nerve and will-power rapidly dissolving.

My primary objective in coming to Spain was to wean my wife away from the temptations of the UK high street. Foolishly, as it now turns out, I thought that Spain had stood still and that there was little more to buy than endless sombreros and straw donkeys, with a few 'I Love Marbella' tee shirts to break up the monotony.

Nothing, tragically, could be further from the truth. Spain seems to have roared into the twenty first century and suddenly gone from a few tawdry flea markets to a horrifying array of brand new shopping centres and sophisticated high streets. I do not think that I have ever seen towns with such a bewildering array of shops and stores. Sadly, it seems, neither has my wife, whose iron determination to look inside each and every one has nearly reduced me to tears.

I have, of course, cunningly reprogrammed the GPS system in our car to bypass any form of habitation in a vain effort to keep the family economy vaguely on track. But, predictably, this has proven useless.

My wife's inability to find her way out of a paper bag seems to reverse itself when it comes to locating shops and particularly boutiques. Using an instinct that is positively primeval, and that in other circumstances would be commendable, she has the precise homing ability of a thirsty camel searching for water in a desert.

There is, of course, a direct inverse relationship between the boosting of the local economy and the traumatic state of my finances. Whilst I am obviously delighted to see Spain doing so well, I am more than a little concerned about how long I can single-handedly sustain their retail industry.

There is also the small matter of Casa Desolada. This has become nothing more than a huge wardrobe with the bathroom, kitchen and bedrooms existing as merely secondary appendages. Needless to say, like most men, my clothes have been relegated to one small drawer and three old metal hangers on the back of the bedroom door.

As to my health and well being, well, I am a mere shadow of my previous self; just another haunted male terrified of those dreadful words: "I am just popping out to the shops…"

Hurricanes, bombs, tsunamis and deadly insects, I cannot take. But UK taxes? I am seriously thinking about it.

A Final Mystery

We live in an astonishing age, with almost every day heralding a new discovery. The human genome project will soon reveal how we all tick, water has been found on distant stars and Big Bang has been traced back to within 10-43 seconds of the event itself. It has even been claimed that scientists are on the point of fathoming the workings of the female mind, with a major breakthrough expected anytime within the next 5,000 years. Happy days, indeed!

However, there remains a deep cloud on the horizon of human knowledge, a mystery that is undoubtedly too profound for the human race to solve at its current rate of evolution. And yet, to many people, finding out the answer is fundamentally important to their wellbeing:

"How is it possible to get building work finished?"

This sublime question has tested some of the finest and most fertile brains of the past 20,000 years. Scientists, of all races and cultures, have struggled desperately to find an answer. In Spain, I have seen renowned philosophers weep publicly in frustration, as they have vainly attempted to intellectualise the staggering complexities of finishing building work. Their courage should be applauded, of course, as publicly discussing this subject is a step way too far for most of us.

Certainly, when the topic of building work has come up around the dinner table at Casa Desolada, it has been met with a hushed and reverent silence. This is only appropriate given the subject matter. Indeed, it is conceivable, and largely accepted now, that the answer to "How to get building work finished?" may only ever be revealed to us in the next world. It is the Holy Grail of Earth's puzzles.

Margaret Denmark

Interestingly, even the high priests of construction, such as architects and surveyors, appear non-plussed. However, like the soothsayers of Delphi, they seem to tolerate their work, whilst subconsciously operating in a different dimension to the rest of us.

Only the other day, I asked an aparajador how long it would take before the work on a friend's villa was completed. He was unable to answer, but his eyes said it all. Blank and impenetrable, they were the eyes of a person who had sat at the right hand of God. This was a man who had experienced all the concentrated tortures and ecstasies life could possibly yield, compacted into the short, working existence of a single, humble human.

I did not press the aparajador. I knew that once he had been on the fringes of a project that was rumoured to have been completed on time. How anyone could survive unchanged after such a powerful mystical experience is beyond me. And it had clearly transformed this modest man, so that now he was rightly and universally revered as a prophet. And yet, there was a haunted aura about him that suggested a tragic fragility, as if another building project could leave him an ethereal memory.

Some people claim that builders never quite finish their work because they would be in direct breach of the laws of evolution, as so clearly set out by the great Charles Darwin himself. It is builders, so some say, who ensure that humankind is constantly tested to the limits. They are, therefore, nature's examiners guaranteeing that only the fittest and strongest survive to pass their more robust genes onto the next generation.

Of course, this line of argument has some merit. Without doubt, for some, the stress entailed in not knowing if their building work will ever be finished is a cause of discomfort. To experience exploding pipes, subsiding walls, leaking roofs and months of unexpectedly waiting in rented accommodation is not for everyone. Indeed, to smile sweetly at a builder you have seen only once or twice, since he started work, can be a little challenging. But this, surely, cannot explain the mystery?

Amazingly, I have even heard some people ignorantly claim that there is no secret to finishing building work. I fear, though, that this is a nonsense circulating amongst the less well educated. Whilst everyone has a democratic right to air their views, to suggest there is no secret, is little more than the bizarre meanderings of deeply warped minds.

For myself, I rather hope that we do not find out the answer to why building work is never finished. Once mankind has solved the riddle of the female mind, we shall need a final mystery to provide our lives with romance and the joy of uncertainty, within our ordered world. Perhaps, in that case, we should be grateful to our builders for their uplifting, and selfless, contribution to all our lives?

The Last Word

Some things, it seems, never change. Indeed, I cannot help feeling that there are more similarities between countries than differences. Frankly, this is not always a good thing.

Take family dynamics, for example, which is a subject very close to my heart. I had always thought that Spain was a macho society and it was this factor that played a compelling part in my decision to come here. I say *my* decision, although, like just about everything else, it was actually my wife's idea and I had little choice in the matter. That said, I did not argue too strongly, as I could see an opening for the speedy assumption of my patriarchal authority.

Certainly, the auguries were good. After all, Spain is nothing if not famous as a macho society. If the publicity is to be believed, the average Spanish man spends virtually all his time taming terrifically powerful stallions in front of his breathlessly adoring and submissive women. On the rare moments that he is not in the saddle, so to speak, he gleefully makes a mockery of the wild power of nature by carelessly dodging enormous fighting bulls. Amazingly, finding a few minutes spare, he will enter a kitchen like a fighting cock and effortlessly knock up a paella, so good it should be Michellin starred.

How could any woman even consider arguing successfully against such a man? Indeed, how could she possibly conceive that she could ever be head of the household? Unthinkable.

The trouble is that my family have yet to see me at my best when tackling wild and powerful forces. The last time I rode, it was on a tiny and very docile pony on Southend beach. True to form, the moment the pony started trotting, I fell off, to the utter derision of my children. As to bulls, they scare the living daylights

Margaret Denmark

out of me and are better admired from behind a very strong fence. I perform slightly better when it comes to cooking, although my credibility took a plunge recently when I burnt a pre-wrapped Mercadonna pizza, after yet again misreading the instructions.

Unfortunately, little of traditional Spain seems to have rubbed off on me so far. More to the point, in no way could I possibly describe my wife as becoming more submissive since living here. And, certainly, 'adoring' would be a gross exaggeration.

Occasionally, in the strictest secrecy, I have discussed my subordinate role with sympathetic British friends of mine. However, when I have urged them to stand firm and be like our Spanish brothers and take command of their women, I have been met by incredulous looks and fits of nervous laughter. This has been swiftly followed by tremulous voices and pale faces, as if we were guilty of discussing some kind of deadly, global terrorist conspiracy. Which, in a way, I suppose, we were.

However, things are never quite what they seem. Recently, I was with a Spanish friend, when I queried the reality of Spanish family life, commenting upon how impressed I was by Spanish machismo. In a British relationship, I said, it was always, and without exception, the woman who had the last word. It had always been like that and, notwithstanding some cataclysm of fantastical proportions, it was highly likely to remain that way.

Downing a large brandy, my friend told me that in Spain it was always the man who had the last word. In fact, it was not the last word but the last two. This sounded promising and I could feel the first embers of a social revolutionary start to glow within me. Perhaps, there was hope after all. Metaphorically speaking, my hands were about to close around the pot of gold at the end of the rainbow.

Once I knew the secret of how to regain man's superiority, I would return immediately to the UK and spread the word or, rather, the two words. I would undoubtedly be treated like an Old Testament prophet by my countrymen and my fame, fortune and happiness would be guaranteed. Already, I could see my place in the history books of the future. Truly, I was on the cusp of a halcyon moment.

"The trouble is," my friend continued, sorrowfully, "our last two words are always: 'Yes, dear'."

So, another illusion was dispelled. I fear there is no hope. Indeed, I suspect that had I spoken to an Islamic potentate in the Middle East, he would have answered much the same way. Perhaps, this explains man's quest to go to the moon. Clearly, only in other worlds will we have the remotest chance of taking charge of our women.

Taking The Heat Was Brought To You By...

Nick Snelling is a writer and professional journalist who lives with his wife and two children in the Valencian mountains of Spain. For further details of Nick's work see: www.nicholassnelling.com

Margaret Denmark is a professional artist who lives in Spain with her partner who is also a painter. For many years she was an illustrator and her work appeared for the Radio Times amongst other national publications. She can be contacted by e-mail on: roycollier22_150@hotmail.com

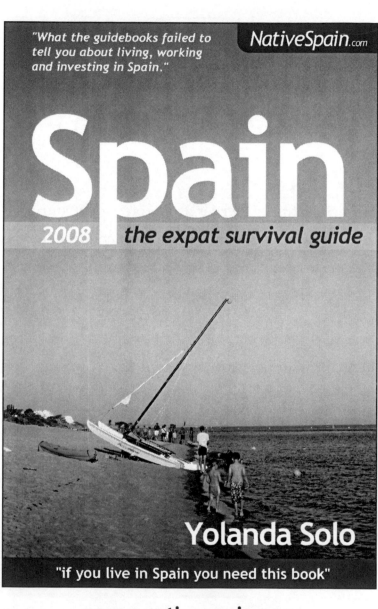

"What the guidebooks failed to tell you about living, working and investing in Spain."

NativeSpain.com

Spain

2008 the expat survival guide

Yolanda Solo

"if you live in Spain you need this book"

www.nativespain.com

NativeSpain.com

Going Native in
Alicante

Susan Bearder

the essential guide to making yourself at home

www.nativespain.com

NativeSpain.com

Going Native in
Catalonia

Simon Harris

the essential guidebook for the inquisitive explorer

www.nativespain.com

Lightning Source UK Ltd.
Milton Keynes UK
12 July 2010

156937UK00001B/18/P